*This planner is specially made for all women bosses!
May all of your plans and goals come into fruition.*

— Brandy Michelle

CONTENT PLANNER

This planner belongs to:

NAME _____

EMAIL _____

PHONE _____

Copyright © 2022 Brandy Michelle

All rights reserved. No portion of this book may be reproduced in any form without permission from the publisher, except as permitted by U.S. copyright law. For permissions contact: emilexdesigns@gmail.com

My Mission

Hello fellow Content Planners! My name is Brandy Michelle. My mission behind creating this content planner is to help eliminate the feeling of being overwhelmed from creating content daily. My hopes are that you will take this planner and learn to create your content monthly, or even weekly versus the stress of trying to create daily. If you use this planner correctly, it will minimize stress and increase productivity.

A plan with consistency is key.

Let's go!

How to use this Content Planner:

On the left-hand side of each calendar sheet, you will see a place to input your month, your monthly theme, along with your monthly business goal. Using a monthly theme always makes it easier to narrow down your daily content topics.

Always set a monthly goal for your business, so that you can assess at the end of each month and readjust goals if need be.

Use the lines on the right side for any notes pertaining to your content ideas, or goals for the month.

Hustle

"To move with a purpose in an intentional direction."

— Brandy Michelle

Month
_____

Theme
_____

Goal
_____

Notes
_____
_____
_____
_____
_____
_____
_____
_____
_____

SUN	MON	TUES	WED	THURS	FRI	SAT

How I Plan to Reach My Monthly Goal

Make it happen girl!

ON YOUR RADAR

#HASHTAGS

WINS

I am calm and focused in all that I do.

Notes

Month
___

Theme
___

Goal
___

SUN	MON	TUES	WED	THURS	FRI	SAT

How I Plan to Reach My Monthly Goal

Make it happen girl!

ON YOUR RADAR

#HASHTAGS

WINS

I know where I am going.

Month

Theme

Goal

Notes

SUN	MON	TUES	WED	THURS	FRI	SAT

How I Plan to Reach My Monthly Goal

Make it happen girl!

ON YOUR RADAR

#HASHTAGS

WINS

All resistance of achieving my goal has vanished.

Notes

Month
_____

Theme
_____

Goal
_____

SUN	MON	TUES	WED	THURS	FRI	SAT

How I Plan to Reach My Monthly Goal

Make it happen girl!

ON YOUR RADAR

#HASHTAGS

WINS

I clearly visualize the attainment of my goals.

Month _____

Theme _____

Goal _____

Notes

_____
_____
_____
_____
_____
_____
_____
_____
_____

SUN	MON	TUES	WED	THURS	FRI	SAT

How I Plan to Reach My Monthly Goal

Make it happen girl!

ON YOUR RADAR

#HASHTAGS

WINS

I have clarity and energy.

Notes

Month
___

Theme
___

Goal
___

SUN	MON	TUES	WED	THURS	FRI	SAT

How I Plan to Reach My Monthly Goal

Make it happen girl!

ON YOUR RADAR

#HASHTAGS

WINS

Being productive brings me joy.

Month

Theme

Goal

Notes

SUN	MON	TUES	WED	THURS	FRI	SAT

How I Plan to Reach My Monthly Goal

Make it happen girl!

ON YOUR RADAR

#HASHTAGS

WINS

I am solution-oriented.

Notes

Month
___

Theme
___

Goal
___

SUN	MON	TUES	WED	THURS	FRI	SAT

How I Plan to Reach My Monthly Goal

Make it happen girl!

ON YOUR RADAR

#HASHTAGS

WINS

I have the tools to manage my time efficiently.

Month
_____

Theme
_____

Goal
_____

Notes
_____
_____
_____
_____
_____
_____
_____
_____
_____

SUN	MON	TUES	WED	THURS	FRI	SAT

How I Plan to Reach My Monthly Goal

Make it happen girl!

ON YOUR RADAR

#HASHTAGS

WINS

I am the master of my own thoughts.

Notes

Month
_____

Theme
_____

Goal
_____

SUN	MON	TUES	WED	THURS	FRI	SAT

How I Plan to Reach My Monthly Goal

Make it happen girl!

ON YOUR RADAR

#HASHTAGS

WINS

I am becoming more organized each day.

Month
_____

Theme
_____

Goal
_____

Notes
_____
_____
_____
_____
_____
_____
_____
_____
_____

SUN	MON	TUES	WED	THURS	FRI	SAT

How I Plan to Reach My Monthly Goal

ON YOUR RADAR

#HASHTAGS

WINS

Make it happen girl!

I am an expert at organizing my tasks.

Notes

Month
___

Theme
___

Goal
___

SUN	MON	TUES	WED	THURS	FRI	SAT

How I Plan to Reach My Monthly Goal

Make it happen girl!

ON YOUR RADAR

#HASHTAGS

WINS

I finish every project I start with enthusiasm.

Thank you!

My hopes are that you used this content planner as a resource to balance your personal and work life. Also, that you were able to eliminate stress by being better organized.

— Brandy Michelle

WOMEN WITH GRACE & HUSTLE